SEARCH THROUGH TIME

TRAVEL THROUGH HISTORY TO FIND LOTS OF FUN THINGS

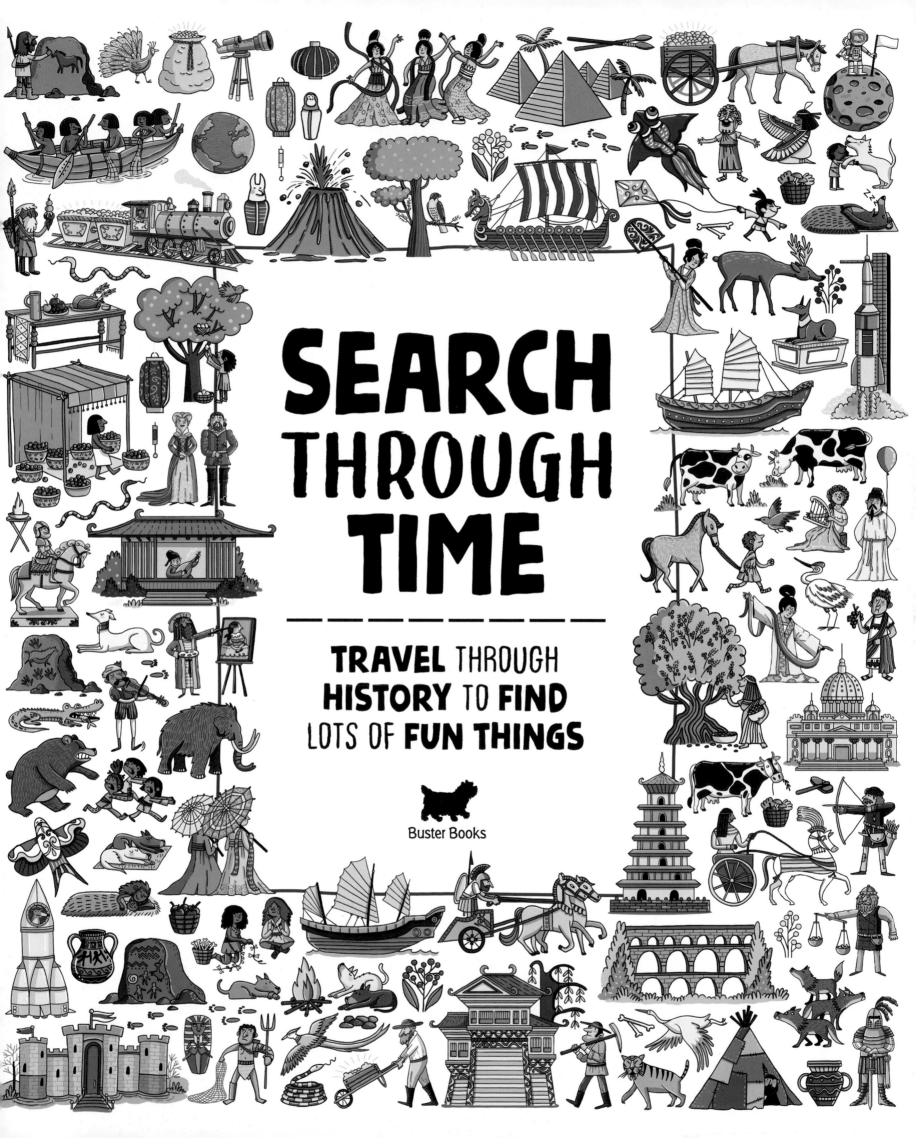

SEARCH THROUGH TIME

TRAVEL THROUGH **HISTORY** TO **FIND** LOTS OF **FUN THINGS**

Buster Books

Illustrated by
Paula Bossio

Written and edited by Emma Taylor
Designed by Zoe Bradley
Cover design by Angie Allison
Historical consultancy by Joe Fullman

First published in Great Britain in 2022 by Buster Books,
an imprint of Michael O'Mara Books Limited, 9 Lion Yard,
Tremadoc Road, London SW4 7NQ

 www.mombooks.com/buster  Buster Books @BusterBooks @buster_books

Copyright © Buster Books 2022

A CIP catalogue record for this book is available from the British Library.

ISBN: 978-1-78055-796-0

1 3 5 7 9 10 8 6 4 2

This book was printed in April 2022 by Leo Paper Products Ltd, Heshan Astros Printing Limited,
Xuantan Temple Industrial Zone, Gulao Town, Heshan City, Guangdong Province, China.

LET THE JOURNEY BEGIN

Prepare to take a magical journey back through history. Meet early humans hunting woolly mammoths, Chinese emperors and people digging for gold in Australia. On your incredible time-travelling adventure you'll see pyramids, palaces and medieval castles. Your journey begins in the Stone Age, many thousands of years ago, and speeds through fascinating civilizations, before blasting into space to reach your final destination – the Space Age.

As you pass through time, your challenge is to search for certain people, animals and objects that belong to each period of history. There are also bonus, modern-day things to look out for – can you find these, too?

Along the way you'll discover amazing facts, figures and firsts about the history of the world.

There are over 150 things to look out for – it's up to you to spot them all!

THE STONE AGE

c.2.6 MILLION YEARS AGO–c.3300 BCE

First you travel to the Stone Age, a time when people hunted giant woolly mammoths and created colourful cave paintings.

CAN YOU FIND ...?

1. A woolly mammoth (an animal with two long tusks).
2. A mother and child sleeping on a bed made of fur.
3. A pair of dogs sleeping by a campfire.
4. A caveman painting a horse.
5. A deer drinking water from a pond.
6. A pack of five wolves out hunting.
7. A gatherer picking apples from a tree.
8. A pair of children running away from a bear.
9. A cavewoman making a necklace from animal bones.
10. A hunter throwing a spear.

Can you spot these bonus, modern-day objects, too?
A. A keyboard B. A football C. An ice cream

Stone Age people developed some of the earliest tools, including simple hammerstones and needles made from bone and ivory.

Woolly mammoths were among the largest land animals and were about as big as modern African elephants. They were hunted for their thick fur and long, curved tusks.

Early humans produced a huge amount of art. The Lascaux Cave in France, for example, contains almost 600 paintings and 1,400 engravings.

Although Stone Age people didn't discover fire, they were the first to control it, using it to heat food and scare away wild animals.

Experts think that Stone Age people were the first to domesticate (tame) dogs and keep them as pets.

The ancient Egyptians worshipped over 2,000 gods and goddesses, including Ra (god of the Sun) and Osiris (god of the afterlife).

The Great Pyramid of Giza is the largest Egyptian pyramid. It is made up of an estimated 2.3 million stone blocks.

Pharaohs' tombs were packed with objects and treasures that they believed they'd need in their next life. Over 5,000 artefacts were found in the tomb of Pharaoh Tutankhamun.

It took around 70 days for the ancient Egyptians to mummify a body to preserve it.

The ancient Egyptian alphabet was made up of roughly 700 pictures and symbols called hieroglyphs. These were usually carved into stone or painted on to wood.

ANCIENT EGYPT

c.3100 BCE–31 BCE

Enter the world of ancient Egypt, a time of ruling pharaohs, giant pyramids and mysterious mummies.

CAN YOU FIND ...?

1. A **black cat** sitting in a **palm tree**.
2. A **pharaoh** in a **purple-and-gold headdress**.
3. **Three fishermen** in a **boat** made of **reeds**.
4. A **market stall** selling **plums**.
5. A **temple** with **hieroglyphs** (symbols) on its **walls**.
6. A **soldier** in a **blue chariot**.
7. A group of **three pyramids**.
8. A **crocodile** eating a **fish**.
9. A **mummy** wrapped in **white bandages**.
10. A **child** riding a **donkey**.

Can you spot these bonus, modern-day objects, too?
A. A mobile phone **B.** A tennis racket **C.** A backpack

ANCIENT GREECE

c.800 BCE–146 BCE

Now you've arrived in ancient Greece. Here, you'll discover crowded theatres, marching soldiers and towering temples.

CAN YOU FIND ...?

1. A **soldier** wearing a **black-and-gold helmet**.
2. A **farmer** collecting **lemons** from a **lemon tree**.
3. A **politician** reading aloud from a **scroll**.
4. An **athlete** with a **discus** (a disc-shaped object).
5. Two **metalworkers** making **tools** inside a **workshop**.
6. **Three actors** wearing **masks**.
7. A **sculptor** carving a **giant marble statue**.
8. **Three** large **orange-and-black clay pots**.
9. A **child** writing on a **wax tablet**.
10. A **bull** wearing a **red collar**.

Can you spot these bonus, modern-day objects, too?
A. A milkshake **B.** A toy car **C.** A pair of headphones

The ancient Greeks invented the theatre. Some cities had theatres that were big enough to hold up to 15,000 people.

The most famous temple in ancient Greece was the Parthenon in Athens. It is estimated that around 13,400 stones were used to build it.

Ancient Greece was made up of over 1,000 city-states, which had their own rulers and sometimes fought each other.

The idea of a democracy was first created by the ancient Greeks. The word itself comes from two Greek words that mean 'rule by the people'.

The ancient Greeks held the world's first Olympic Games in 776 BCE. Events included boxing, wrestling and chariot racing.

Ancient Rome was ruled by emperors for over 400 years. Augustus Caesar was the first and longest-reigning Emperor of Rome.

The Colosseum is a giant, 50,000 seat open-air theatre in Rome. It took eight years to complete and over 997,000 tonnes (1 million tons) of stone and concrete were used to build it.

The Romans built around 80,000 kilometres (50,000 miles) of road, reaching as far as North Africa. Some of the same routes are still in use today.

Roman soldiers were made to serve in the army for 25 years. Some of them had to march up to 30 kilometres (20 miles) a day.

The Circus Maximus was the first and largest stadium built in ancient Rome. It was built for chariot races and could seat around 250,000 people.

ANCIENT ROME

753 BCE–476 CE

Next up is ancient Rome, Italy, where emperors feast, chariots race and gladiators fight.

CAN YOU FIND ...?

1. A **gladiator** holding a **trident** (fishing spear) and a **net**.
2. An **emperor** wearing a **purple toga**.
3. A group of **three people** bathing inside a **bath house**.
4. **Four plates** of grapes.
5. An **erupting volcano**.
6. A **musician** playing a **drum**.
7. **Three** pots of **gold coins**.
8. A **mosaic** (a pattern made from coloured stones) of a **fish**.
9. A **brown dog** drinking water from a **fountain**.
10. A group of **three children** playing with **wooden swords**.

Can you spot these bonus, modern-day objects, too?
A. A pair of rollerskates **B.** A disco ball **C.** A camera

THE TANG DYNASTY

618–907 CE

You have reached China during the Tang Dynasty – a period of time known as a golden age for invention, art, music and writing.

CAN YOU FIND ...?

1. **15** exploding **fireworks**.
2. A **woman** holding a **gold mirror**.
3. A group of **five dancers**.
4. A **big red kite** with **eyes**.
5. An **emperor** wearing a **brown robe** sitting in a **gold chair**.
6. A **woman** carrying a **blue-and-yellow umbrella**.
7. A **musician** playing a wooden **flute**.
8. A **yellow-and-red** hanging **lantern**.
9. A **sailing boat** with **square-shaped sails**.
10. A **camel** carrying **packages** on its back.

Can you spot these bonus, modern-day objects, too?
A. A pink balloon **B.** A pair of sunglasses **C.** A paper aeroplane

Chang'an, the Tang capital, had a marketplace with thousands of shops that sold all kinds of things, from jewellery and musical instruments to medicine and spices.

The world's first mechanical clock was invented in 725 CE by a Buddhist monk and mathematician, Yi Xing. It was powered by water dripping on to a wheel, which made a full turn every 24 hours.

The people of ancient China were the first to develop woodblock printing, a technique used to print images and text on to paper. The *Diamond Sutra* is the oldest surviving printed book and dates back to 868 CE.

Wu Zhao was the first and only female emperor in Chinese history. She came to power in 690 CE and ruled for 15 years.

Calligraphy, the art of handwriting, was an important skill in ancient China. Calligraphers would practise for years learning to draw over 40,000 different characters.

The Vikings were among the greatest explorers in the ancient world. They sailed all the way from their home in Scandinavia and across the Atlantic Ocean to the coast of North America.

The Vikings were expert boat builders. The Gokstad, one of the largest Viking ships ever found, was 24 metres (78 feet) long and big enough to fit 32 oarsmen with 16 oars on each side.

Viking people were the first to use skiis for fun, not just for transport. The skiis were usually made from wood and oiled with animal fat to help them slide through the snow.

When Vikings died, they were sometimes buried with everything that they might need in their next life – from new clothes and jewellery to weapons and even furniture.

The Vikings used an alphabet made up of 16 letters called 'runes', which they carved into pieces of bone, wood and stone. Over 3,000 runic engravings have been found, mainly in Scandinavia.

THE VIKINGS

793–1066 CE

Welcome to the age of the Vikings. Here, you'll find impressive longships, seafaring warriors and fearsome conquerors.

CAN YOU FIND ...?

1. An **archer** with a **bow and arrow**.
2. A **longship** with a **red-and-white sail**.
3. A **warrior** with a **round shield** and an **axe**.
4. A **falcon** sitting in a **tree**.
5. A **large runestone** (a stone with writing carved into it).
6. A **woman** cooking food in a **cauldron**.
7. A **group** of **three children** fishing in a **pond**.
8. A **farmer** picking **vegetables**.
9. **Eight deer**.
10. A **market stall** selling **fabrics**.

Can you spot these bonus, modern-day objects, too?
A. A teddy bear **B.** An electric guitar **C.** A skateboard

THE MIDDLE AGES

c.500–1500 CE

You've now arrived in the Middle Ages, a time in European
history filled with jousting knights and magnificent castles.

CAN YOU FIND ...?

1. A **knight** holding a **round shield** with a **sun** on it.
2. A **guard** keeping watch inside a **watchtower**.
3. A **queen** wearing a **red gown**.
4. A **flaming arrow** soaring through the **sky**.
5. A **musician** playing a **buisine** (a long trumpet).
6. A **shepherd** herding a flock of **five sheep**.
7. A **castle** with a **green-and-yellow checked flag**.
8. A **court jester** in an **orange-and-purple costume**.
9. Two **knights** on **horseback** jousting with **lances** (long spears).
10. A **child** wearing a **red hat** collecting water from a **well**.

Can you spot these bonus, modern-day objects, too?
A. A pink umbrella **B.** A hairdryer **C.** A blue handbag

Longbows were among the most powerful weapons of the Middle Ages. Longbowmen could shoot arrows over 200 metres (650 feet) and could fire at least six arrows in a minute.

Knights of the Middle Ages would train for around 15 years and began their training as young as seven or eight years old.

Between 1347 and 1351, a mysterious plague called the Black Death swept across Europe. It killed over 20 million people – over one-third of Europe's whole population.

Jousting was a popular sport where knights competed to knock each other off their horse. Knights could collide at speeds of over 48 kilometres per hour (30 miles per hour).

During the Middle Ages, knights' armour became increasingly thick and heavy. A whole suit of armour could weigh up to 50 kilograms (110 pounds).

The Renaissance was a time of exploration and discovery. An important expedition was that of Christopher Columbus, an Italian explorer, who sailed to the Americas in 1492.

The Gutenberg press, a mechanical device used to print words on to paper, was created by Johannes Gutenberg, a German inventor, in the 1430s. This meant that books could be printed far quicker and cheaper than ever before.

The *Mona Lisa*, one of the world's most famous paintings, was painted during the Renaissance by Leonardo da Vinci. It took him 20 years to complete.

Galileo Galilei, an Italian astronomer and mathematician, developed a telescope that could magnify (enlarge) things up to 30 times their original size.

William Shakespeare was a popular playwright, poet and actor who was born during the Renaissance. Throughout his lifetime, he penned over 150 poems and at least 37 plays.

THE RENAISSANCE

c.1300–c.1660

Your next stop is the Renaissance. 'Renaissance' means 'rebirth' in French as there was a new interest in ancient Greece and Rome during this time.

CAN YOU FIND ...?

1. An **artist** painting a **portrait**.
2. **Two people** playing a game of **chess**.
3. A **ship** with **blue and white flags**.
4. A **dancer** performing on a **stage**.
5. An **astronomer** in a **purple robe** using a **telescope**.
6. A **musician** playing a **violin**.
7. A **palace** with **two turrets** (towers).
8. A **ginger cat** sleeping by a **fire**.
9. A **scholar** (pupil) in a **red cloak** reading a **book**.
10. **Three peacocks**.

Can you spot these bonus, modern-day objects, too?
A. A pink doughnut **B.** A yellow suitcase **C.** A pepperoni pizza

THE AUSTRALIAN GOLD RUSHES

1851–1914

Now explore the Australian Gold Rushes. A 'gold rush' is when lots of people suddenly turn up at a newly discovered goldfield.

CAN YOU FIND ...?

1. A **pair** of **children** poking their heads out from a **tent**.
2. A **woman** in a **blue dress** chopping **wood**.
3. Ten **sacks** of **gold nuggets**.
4. A **white horse** pulling along a **wagon** filled with bales of **hay**.
5. A **miner** in a **brown hat** carrying a **pickaxe**.
6. A **cabin** with **pink curtains**.
7. Four **red lanterns**.
8. A **mother** and **baby koala**.
9. A **woman** in a **yellow dress** reading a **newspaper**.
10. A **grey dog** hiding behind a **barrel**.

Can you spot these bonus, modern-day objects, too?

A. A rainbow-coloured lollipop **B.** A television **C.** A snorkel

Hundreds of thousands of people, nicknamed 'diggers', came from all over Australia, as well as China, Great Britain, Poland, Germany and even California to seek their fortune.

The biggest gold nugget ever found was in Victoria in 1868. It weighed 72 kilograms (159 pounds) – that's almost as heavy as an adult kangaroo.

At Mount Alexander, Victoria, about 110,000 kilograms (240,000 pounds) of gold was found in the first two years of one gold rush, between 1851 and 1853.

In the 1850s, the gold found in Victoria made up more than a third of the whole world's gold production.

Between 1851 and 1871, the Australian population grew from 438,000 people to 1.7 million, as people flocked to find gold.

In 1957, the Soviet Union launched the first man-made satellite (a spaceship that can orbit the Earth), Sputnik 1. It was about the size of a beach ball.

In 1969, American astronauts Neil Armstrong and Edwin 'Buzz' Aldrin travelled just over 400,000 kilometres (250,000 miles) to become the first people on the Moon.

The International Space Station is a spacecraft that is about the size of an American football field. It's the biggest man-made object to orbit Earth, circling our planet every 90 minutes at around 28,000 kilometres per hour (17,500 miles per hour).

An astronaut's space suit can weigh around 130 kilograms (280 pounds) just on its own. That's almost as heavy as an adult panda.

NASA, America's space agency, has sent five rovers (wheeled space-exploration vehicles) to Mars since the 1990s. The latest rover, sent in 2021, is the largest and most advanced ever sent to another planet.

THE SPACE AGE

1957–PRESENT DAY

Are you ready? It's now time to blast off into the Space Age.
Here, you'll see awesome astronauts, exciting planets and
all kinds of space technology.

CAN YOU FIND ...?

1. A **rocket scientist** using a **computer**.
2. A pair of **children** watching a **black-and-white television**.
3. An **astronaut** wearing a **gold helmet**.
4. A **red-and-white space shuttle** getting ready to launch.
5. A **brown astrodog** sitting inside a **spacecraft**.
6. A **scientist** looking through a **blue telescope**.
7. A **silver satellite** with **four antennas** (long rods).
8. An **asteroid** (space rock) colliding with a **red planet**.
9. An **astronaut** with a **green flag**, stepping on to the **Moon**.
10. A **space telescope** going around **Earth**.

Can you spot these bonus, futuristic objects, too?
A. A flying car **B.** A pair of rocket shoes **C.** A hoverboard

ALL THE ANSWERS (AND SOME BONUS FACTS)

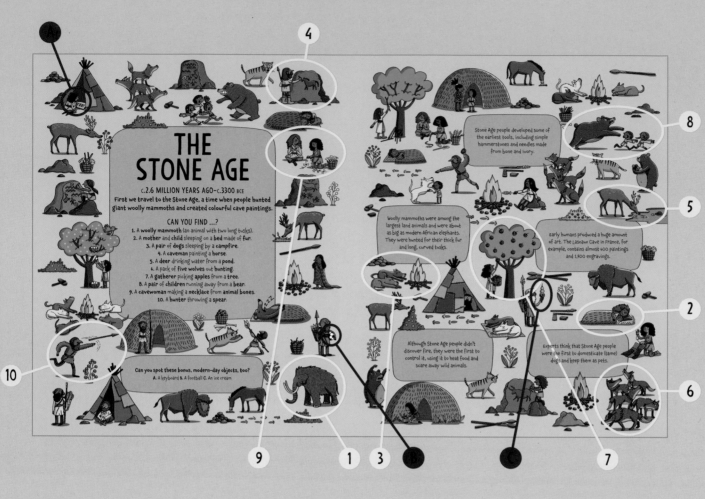

THE STONE AGE

c.2.6 MILLION YEARS AGO–c.3300 BCE

First we travel to the Stone Age, a time when people hunted giant woolly mammoths and created colourful cave paintings.

CAN YOU FIND ...?

1. A woolly mammoth (an animal with two long tusks).
2. A mother and child sleeping on a bed made of fur.
3. A pair of dogs sleeping by a campfire.
4. A caveman painting a horse.
5. A deer drinking water from a pond.
6. A pack of five wolves out hunting.
7. A gatherer picking apples from a tree.
8. A pair of children running away from a bear.
9. A cavewoman making a necklace from animal bones.
10. A hunter throwing a spear.

Can you spot these bonus, modern-day objects, too?
A. A keyboard B. A football C. An ice cream

Stone Age people developed some of the earliest tools, including simple hammerstones and needles made from bone and ivory.

Woolly mammoths were among the largest land animals and were about as big as modern African elephants. They were hunted for their thick fur and long, curved tusks.

Early humans produced a huge amount of art. The Lascaux Cave in France, for example, contains almost 400 paintings and 1,500 engravings.

Although Stone Age people didn't discover fire, they were the first to control it, using it to heat food and scare away wild animals.

Experts think that Stone Age people were the first to domesticate (tame) dogs and keep them as pets.

Stonehenge is a circle of stones in England built by the people of the Stone Age and early Bronze Age. Some of the stones weigh a whopping 22 tonnes (24 tons).

During the Stone Age, people in Egypt became the first farmers, while in other parts of the world, people were still hunting wild animals and picking wild vegetables and fruits.

The bandages of an unwrapped mummy could stretch for 1.6 kilometres (1 mile).

The ancient Egyptians came up with their own versions of many things we use today, such as paper, pens, locks and keys.

The ancient Egyptians worshipped over 2,000 gods and goddesses, including Ra (god of the Sun) and Osiris (god of the afterlife).

The Great Pyramid of Giza is the largest Egyptian pyramid. It is made up of an estimated 2.3 million stone blocks.

Pharaohs' tombs were packed with objects and treasures that they believed they'd need in their next life. Over 5,000 artefacts were found in the tomb of Pharaoh Tutankhamun.

It took around 70 days for the ancient Egyptians to mummify a body to preserve it.

The ancient Egyptian alphabet was made up of roughly 700 pictures and symbols called hieroglyphs. These were usually carved into stone or painted on to wood.

ANCIENT EGYPT

c.3100 BCE–31 BCE

Enter the world of ancient Egypt, a time of ruling pharaohs, giant pyramids and mysterious mummies.

CAN YOU FIND ...?

1. A black cat sitting in a palm tree.
2. A pharaoh in a purple-and-gold headdress.
3. Three fishermen in a boat made of reeds.
4. A market stall selling plums.
5. A temple with hieroglyphs (symbols) on its walls.
6. A soldier in a blue chariot.
7. A group of three pyramids.
8. A crocodile eating a fish.
9. A mummy wrapped in white bandages.
10. A child riding a donkey.

Can you spot these bonus, modern-day objects, too?
A. A mobile phone B. A tennis racket C. A backpack

It is believed that a man named Pheidippides ran 42 kilometres (26 miles) from the town of Marathon to Athens to report that the Greek army had won a great battle. This is where the name and distance of today's marathon race comes from.

The city-state Sparta was well-known for its strong army of men. Spartan boys trained to become warriors from as young as seven years old.

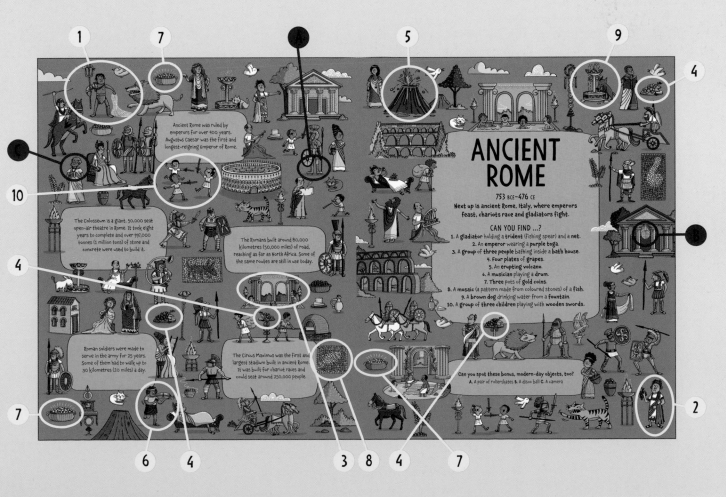

The people of ancient Rome built a system of bridges called aqueducts to carry water to the city. Over 500 years, 11 aqueducts were built, bringing water from as far as 92 kilometres (57 miles) away.

Rome was the first city in the world to record a population of 1 million people.

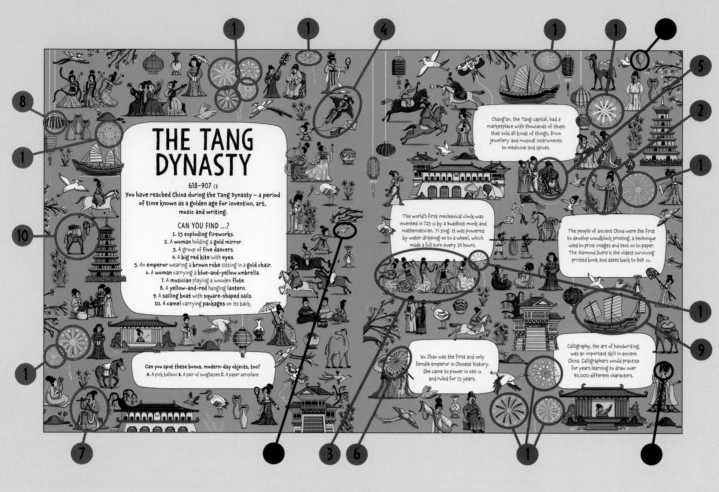

Poetry became very popular during the Tang era. Around 50,000 poems by about 200 authors have survived to the modern day from this period.

It is estimated that during the Tang Dynasty, China had the largest population of any country. According to a census (survey) in 742 CE, there were between 50 and 60 million people living there.

THE TANG DYNASTY

618–907 CE

You have reached China during the Tang Dynasty – a period of time known as a golden age for invention, art, music and writing.

CAN YOU FIND ...?

1. 15 exploding fireworks.
2. A woman holding a gold mirror.
3. A group of five dancers.
4. A big red kite with eyes.
5. An emperor wearing a brown robe sitting in a gold chair.
6. A woman carrying a blue-and-yellow umbrella.
7. A musician playing a wooden flute.
8. A yellow-and-red hanging lantern.
9. A sailing boat with square-shaped sails.
10. A camel carrying packages on its back.

Can you spot these bonus, modern-day objects, too?
A. A pink balloon B. A pair of sunglasses C. A paper aeroplane

Chang'an, the Tang capital, had a marketplace with thousands of shops that sold all kinds of things, from jewellery and musical instruments to medicine and spices.

The world's first mechanical clock was invented in 725 CE by a Buddhist monk and mathematician, Yi Xing. It was powered by water dripping on to a wheel, which made a full turn every 24 hours.

The people of ancient China were the first to develop woodblock printing, a technique used to print images and text on to paper. The Diamond Sutra is the oldest surviving printed book and dates back to 848 CE.

Wu Zhao was the first and only female emperor in Chinese history. She came to power in 690 CE and ruled for 15 years.

Calligraphy, the art of handwriting, was an important skill in ancient China. Calligraphers would practise for years learning to draw over 40,000 different characters.

The Vikings were known for their good hygiene. They generally bathed at least once a week, which was a lot more than many other people at the time.

The Vikings tended to eat only two meals a day. They were known as 'dagmal' and 'nattmal', which meant 'day meal' and 'night meal'.

THE VIKINGS

793–1066 CE

Welcome to the age of the Vikings. Here, you'll find impressive longships, seafaring warriors and fearsome conquerors.

CAN YOU FIND ...?

1. An archer with a bow and arrow.
2. A longship with a red-and-white sail.
3. A warrior with a round shield and an axe.
4. A falcon sitting in a tree.
5. A large runestone (a stone with writing carved into it).
6. A woman cooking food in a cauldron.
7. A group of three children fishing in a pond.
8. A farmer picking vegetables.
9. Eight deer.
10. A market stall selling fabrics.

Can you spot these bonus, modern-day objects, too?
A. A teddy bear B. An electric guitar C. A skateboard

The Vikings were among the greatest explorers in the ancient world. They sailed all the way from their home in Scandinavia and across the Atlantic Ocean to the coast of North America.

The Vikings were expert boat builders. The Gokstad, one of the largest Viking ships ever found, was 24 metres (78 feet) long and big enough to fit 32 oarsmen with 16 oars on each side.

Viking people were the first to use skis for fun, not just for transport. The skis were usually made from wood and oiled with animal fat to help them slide through the snow.

When Vikings died, they were sometimes buried with everything that they might need in their next life – from new clothes and jewellery to weapons and even furniture.

The Vikings used an alphabet made up of 16 letters called 'runes', which they carved into pieces of bone, wood and stone. Over 3,000 rune engravings have been found, mainly in Scandinavia.

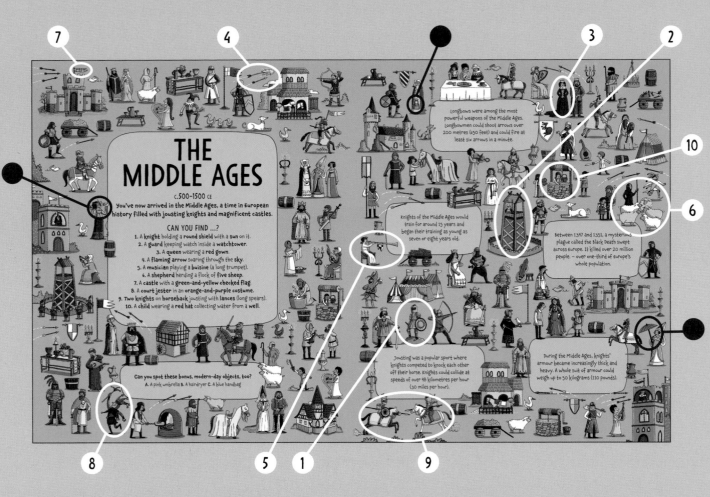

The first pair of glasses were invented during the Middle Ages. They were used for reading and had to be held by hand.

In the Middle Ages, animals, including even insects, could be put on trial if they were suspected of committing a crime. There are records of at least 85 animal trials that took place during this time.

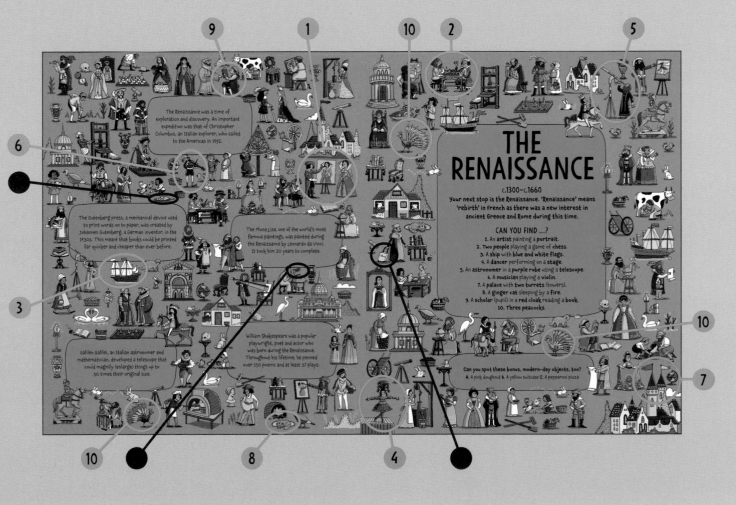

The first public library opened in Italy in 1452. Up until then, libraries could only be used by selected people.

Ballet started in the royal courts of Renaissance Italy. By 1661, Paris in France had its own ballet school and the dance moved to the stage.

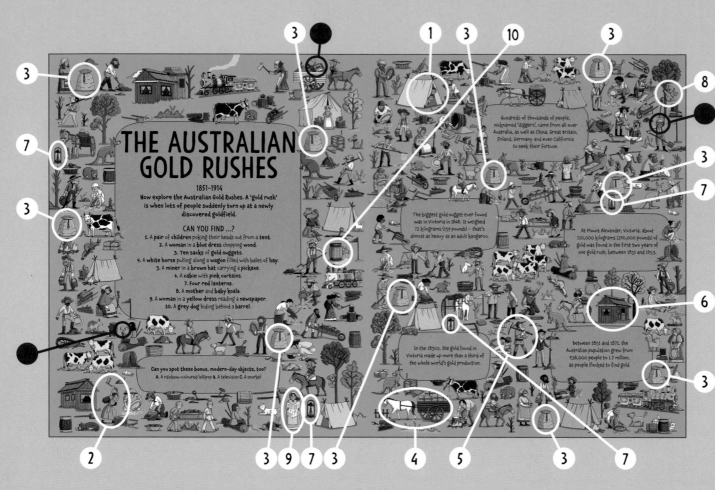

The Boddington Gold Mine is the biggest gold mine in Australia. Discovered in the 1890s, more than 1.7 million kilograms (3.75 million pounds) of gold has been mined there.

In 1882, Edwin and Thomas Morgan made one of Australia's most important gold discoveries at Ironside Mountain. It was one of Queensland's longest-surviving gold mines, with work continuing at the site until 1981.

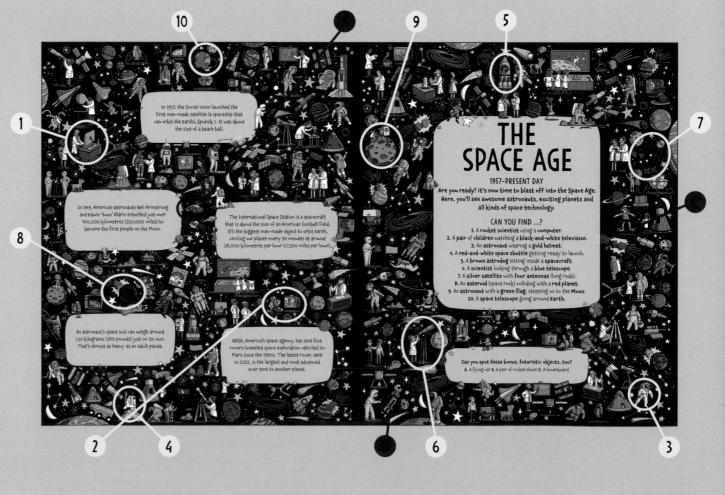

In 1963, Russian cosmonaut Valentina Tereshkova became the first woman in space. She was chosen from 400 other candidates and was only 26 years old when she made her space flight.

The first animals in space were fruit flies sent up in a rocket in 1947.